How to fill **50** jobs
in **90** days

The recruitment blueprint for people, profit and position

Heike Guilford

Note To Readers

This publication is designed to provide accurate, helpful and informative material in regard to the subject matter covered. The suggested tools and strategies covered in this book may not be suitable to everyone, and are not guaranteed or warranted to produce any particular results.

This book is sold with the understanding that the author is not engaged in rendering legal, financial, accounting, or other professional advice or services. If legal advice or other expert assistance is required, the services of a competent professional should be sought.

The author does not take responsibility for any liability, loss or risk, personal or otherwise, which is incurred as a consequence, directly or indirectly, of the use and application of any of the contents of this book.

This publication may not be reproduced, stored in a retrieval system, or transmitted in whole or in part, in any form or by any means, electronic, mechanical, photocopying, recording, or otherwise, without the prior written permission of the author.

Contents

In 2015 I was nominated for a Nursing Times Leaders Award by **Daniel Marsden** (Practice Development Nurse for People with learning disabilities at East Kent Hospitals University NHS Foundation Trust). He had the following to say about me:

"During the past two years Heike has faced significant challenges not only with personal health issues, but also with her decision to take the isolating action of whistleblowing on an employer regarding resourcing and staffing issues at her practice that impacted on the effectiveness of the care provided to people with severe learning disabilities, autism, and behaviours that challenge.

"These issues culminated in Heike being made redundant, an experience that caused her to reflect on her toolbox of personal qualities that she was then able to call upon to take a stand for herself and the people she worked with and advocated for. She chose to invest her time and resources into a Neuro-linguistic Programming and Coaching courses and set herself up in business to support other nurses to develop their own toolboxes to achieve the things that they desire for their nursing careers. The result was the launch of 'The Coaching Nurse' at the end of 2014.

In May 2015, Heike hosted a Learning Disability Leadership conference, to which local, regional, and national nursing leaders were invited to speak. The conference was peppered with workshop activities to encourage participants to consider what they might dream of for their careers and those of the people they manage and influence.

Heike has received a number of invitations to speak at regional and national conferences, authored on her subject, and hosted Twitter chats to help nurses develop their tool boxes of resources to develop resilience and leadership."

Daniel Marsden, 2015

CHAPTER ONE
How nearly dying solved my staffing troubles

I was in the midst of a full blown recruitment campaign with application forms piling high on my desk. One minute I was trying to decide who to invite for recruitment day, and the next I was fighting for my life.

I woke up with horrific pain shooting through my left leg on 16th January 2014. I could see that my leg had swollen to what can only be described as elephant size. Hospital tests revealed an ovarian tumour compressing a vein in my leg, causing deep vein thrombosis. I needed lifesaving surgery and extensive medical treatment.

I felt a wave of relief wash over me when my cancer tests came back clear. I was looking forward to return back to normal. It did not turn out that way. I was informed in my Return To Work meeting that my position would cease to exist, so I chose to take redundancy. It was like someone had hijacked my life and left me at the side of the road. I decided to invest a large chunk of my savings into coaching courses to help me get back on my feet. It worked! When I completed my courses I felt inspired and excited to share my newfound skills. I opened the doors to 'The Coaching Nurse' in the summer of 2014.

While I never dreamed of running my own business before, I was ready to embrace this new adventure. There was just one problem: I did not have any clients! I started to read countless books on sales, marketing and networking. I discovered the stories behind well-loved brands from Apple to Zappos. I spent night after night studying how I could apply the success strategies from Brendon Burchard, Steve Jobs, Richard Branson or Anthony Robbins to my business. My business began to thrive. I started presenting my work at local -and national events . I organised my own conference with Dr. Ben Thomas from the Department of Health as the keynote speaker and I even got the chance to write guest blogs for national publications such as the RCNi journal.

One night, I went to a talk about the financial meltdown about to hit the healthcare sector. I decided to look into this more and discovered that billions of pounds are lost each year to agency fees. I realised that everything I've learned could be used to save cash and find the right people for the job.

Soon after, I secured funding from Health Education England to create staff recruitment -and retention courses. HR professionals and clinicians attending my courses got many new ideas to support cost effective recruitment.

The success of the courses inspired me to share my work and give you new inspiration for your recruitment campaigns in healthcare today.

Just a short disclaimer before we start: Coaching is all about the tools. You will learn many strategies you can use to completely innovate and transform recruitment in your service. They will only be effective if you are committed to using them. This may seem totally obvious to you. However, I know how things can pan out when you have tools and high expectations. There were times when I bought the Ferrari of running shoes just to be left disappointed when they did not turn me into Speedy Gonzales overnight. I learned that mastery requires the willingness to learn, explore and stay committed.

After learning of a Clinical Manager using my system to slash his agency bills down to zero, building a pipeline of potential candidates and increasing brand exposure, I just had to share this blueprint with you.

What you will learn in this book:

This book will give you everything you need to plan out a powerful recruitment campaign. I have designed a blueprint to help you ditch agency staff and fill your jobs in 90 days. The LEAN Recruitment framework takes you through how to LOCATE the right person for the job, how to ENGAGE your future workforce, how to ASSESS your candidates and how to NEGOTIATE the best deal for you.

Who this book is for:

This book is for you if saving money on staff recruitment -and retention is part of your job description.

How to use this book:

I know from own experience that your diary is already bulging with appointments, requests and conflicting demands. You may not have the time to read this book from cover -to cover. You don't have to. Each chapter contains short protocols with everything you need to get started straight away. I have put together a variety of ideas, so that you can choose the ones most relevant to you, your business and your situation. This gives you the freedom to take the best and leave the rest!

Let's get started!

How a bottle of champagne turned into a million quid...

How often do you get excited about financial reviews and can't wait to present your numbers? Unless you are an accountant with a love for numbers or you've hit all your financial goals, the answer is likely to be never. I remember the time I went in to present my KPI figures with a spring in my step. I could not wait to see the smile on people's faces when I told them good news for a change. Staffing levels reaching full complement, agency expenditure down to zero and dropping absence levels would be all music to my colleagues' ears.

The announcement of a service development due to open in four short months, requiring 17 Qualified Nurses and 33 Support Work staff barely registered. A wave of shock and despair shot through me.

Where would I find that number of people wanting to work in a challenging behaviour unit in a matter of weeks?

"Recruit 50 people in 90 days without using an agency and I will give you a bottle of champagne!" My boss Tony knew me too well. He was well aware that I like nothing better than a good challenge coming my way. It worked! My confidence soared and ideas how to get started were already buzzing through my mind on the short trip to sell this new project to my team.

Our marketing campaign included colleagues giving presentations at universities, existing staff leading presentations and pitches on recruitment days, ads in local papers, cards at newsagents, a bonus referral scheme, pitching vacancies to temporary agency staff and setting up an international student project.

Our focus shifted to our assessment and selection process once applications began to trickle in. We developed a form evaluating the attitude, qualifications and skills of clients based on a fair scoring system. Interviews included a number of scenario questions to draw out candidate's values and beliefs. Involving clients and colleagues from every department in team-assessment exercises gave everyone the chance to see if we were right for each other. Every activity was designed to reduce the risk of staff leaving and improving our prospects of success. Opening my office door ninety days later, there it was: one shiny bottle of champagne!

We managed to retain all directly recruited members of staff for over 12 months. This turned into a total cost saving of over £1million in the months to come.

Profit Myths Debunked

There is a myth in healthcare that refuses to die and goes something like this: all you need for a thriving service is clients, a good relationship with parents and commissioners and a unique selling point to outshine your competition. Once you have all these things in place, it's time to quickly recruit a staff team and watch profits roll in. Of course, it never happens like this. Your expected profits get eaten up by agency fees, you need to discover the potion to cure the frequent spikes of sickness-and absence rates. The magic staff cupboard is still out for delivery, hence you end up short staffed every time supportive observations increase. Suddenly, it's more than just your budget feeling the drain. Morale is low, applications are drying up and the scores on the doors have morphed into an action plan as long as your arm.

The simple truth: profit does not come from clients alone. Profit will be generated once you have cash left over after covering all your cost bases. I know you might be wondering why I am telling you this, when this seems completely obvious to you. I have learned from experience that not everyone knows the biggest expense in any service comes from the staff bill. I have witnessed colleagues following the lure of the money -AKA more clients - just to find their profits swimming away with every safeguarding incident or resignation letter.

It is my belief that there is a war for talent raging. To win the war, you will need to value staff as the greatest asset in your service and recognise HR for what it truly is: the beating heart at the centre of your operation.

Why Recruitment Is Cash In The Bank

How much cash will arrive in your bank account once you ditch the agency and fill your jobs in 90 days?

Qualified staff
Estimated agency fees for 17 RN temporary shift cover over 12 months:

Rates: £19.50 per hour/per person
Cost of covering 1x12 hour shift: £234
Average number of shifts per month needing agency cover: 12
Cost of 1 agency RN covering 12 shifts per month = £2,808
Cost of 1 agency RN over 12 months = £33,696
Cost of 17 agency RN's over 12 months = £572,832

Cost of 17 directly recruited Staff Nurses with an annual salary of £27,000 =£459,000
Cash saved in one year ditching agency staff and commission fees of £5,000 p.p **=£198,832**

Care staff:
£10.50 per hour/per person
Cost of covering 1x12hour shift: £126
Average number of shifts per month needing agency cover: 12
Cost of 1 agency SW covering 12 shifts per month: £1512
Cost of 1 agency SW over 12 months = £18,144
Cost of 33 agency SW covering 12 months= £598,752

Cost of 33 Support Workers on £8/h over the year: £456,192
Estimated cost savings total over 12 months = **£142,560**

Total cost savings from ditching agency staff per year: **£341,392**

Cash in the bank 36 months from now: £1,024176

Not all your staff will know the ins and outs of corporate finance. Find free tools to engage your workforce into every aspect of your business here: www.goagencyfree.com

CHAPTER TWO
When The Five Year Forward View Meets Hollywood

Doomsday is looming. Services are in danger of being swallowed up by a huge black financial hole. You can see long queues of people, all desperate for your help. They are the lucky ones. Rapid advances in technology and science mean you are able to save them. Word has spread of your excellent service. Expectations for you to deliver on your promise are high. Just as you are about to open your doors, men in black arrive. Your heart is thumping hard in your chest, as they slowly reveal what's in their briefcase.

Spreadsheets with red ink all over them. Numbers telling you that agency usage, sickness cover and spending £30k every time you needed to replace just one member of staff have taken its toll. Just as you think it can't get any worse, disaster strikes. "Come up with a plan to save cash, improve productivity and deliver better quality. The code name will be Sustainable Transformation Plans or STP's for short. Get it done or suffer the consequences."

"Which are?" If looks could freeze, you would have turned into an ice sculpture by now. "If you fail, we will take away a large chunk of your cash. If you keep missing your targets, we'll have to put you in financial special measures. You will put an announcement on your website telling people you couldn't cut it. You'll have to shake things up around here. Give your services a make-over. Get people to work together. Use apprenticeship schemes to build career pathways. Remember your service is a business at the end of the day. Treat it like one. We'll be back."

When the shock finally wears off, you gather your team together for a crisis meeting. Putting together all the clues you have so far, leads you to one surprising conclusion. When you start treating all areas of your service as a business, doesn't that also mean that every single one of them has potential to make profit? Businesses in the open market use sophisticated marketing -and sales strategies to attract the right people there to stay into their door. Your whole workforce have serious sales skills already. The care worker convincing a client to stick with a new care plan. The Practitioner persuading colleagues to bury the hatched. The manager telling the story of their career progression to applicants. Everyone is already in sales -and marketing. All you've got to do now is figure out what other people operating in a crowded market do to win profits and people.

CHAPTER THREE
How To Locate People

How To Determine Your Value In The Market

Your goals:

- To define and track your value in a competitive market place
- To determine how your job vacancy compares to your rivals
- To map out a strategy to gain competitive advantages

SWOT analysis

Definition: "SWOT, which stands for strengths, weaknesses, opportunities and threats, is an analytical framework that can help your company face its greatest challenges and finds its most promising markets. The method was created in the 1960s by business gurus Edmund P. Learned, C. Rowland Christensen, Kenneth Andrews and William D. Brook in their book "Business Policy, Text and Cases" (R.D Irwin, 1969)" Nicole Fallon Taylor

How to go about it:

Consider possible Strengths:

- What do you consider to be your biggest strengths compared to your competitors?
- What do you consider your best selling points?
- What training package do you currently offer?
- What childcare benefits do you offer?
- Have you got good local transport links to your workplace? Are there shops nearby?
- How does the training you offer support the future careers of your staff?
- Do you have staff actively involved in apprenticeship schemes?
- Do you have links with local universities, voluntary organisations and colleges?
- Do you offer support for qualified Practitioners with NMC re-validation?
- Do you train staff in developing specialist skills in areas of interest? Examples: short mentorship courses, Cognitive Behaviour Therapy, Positive Behaviour Support, Leadership-and management, etc.
- Do you have a blog on your website?
- Do you have structured plans in place to support career progression in addition to your appraisal systems?
- Do you have positive and realistic testimonials from staff members, clients and families in your marketing materials?
- Do you have favourable regulatory review reports?
- What is the average length of stay for one member of staff?
- Do you give staff the opportunity to engage with the wider nursing –and care community? This may include giving presentations, leading student placements, writing a guest blog or newsletter article, Social Media links with like-minded professionals via Twitter, LinkedIn or Facebook Groups

Consider possible weaknesses:

- Is your organisation difficult to access via public transport links or based in a remote location?
- Are you concerned about your CQC 'Scores on doors' or other negative reviews?
- How does your salary and benefits compare to services in the local vicinity?
- Do you have a Social Media engagement strategy in place?
- Are your employees at risk of suffering workplace injuries on a frequent basis?
- Do you have high staff turnover rates?
- Do you cover a significant number of open vacancies with agency staff?
- Do you feel isolated from government supported networks?

Consider possible opportunities:

- Development of career progression plans using new apprenticeship schemes
- Offering free career clinics to staff
- Developing a strategy to convert agency into regular staff
- Developing a clear strategy to showcase the benefits of working within the service involving your existing staff team
- Designing a marketing plan aimed at setting yourself apart from your competitors in terms of workforce development, other words creating your own Unique Selling Point (USP) for staff

Consider possible threats:

- Current workforce crisis across the nursing –and care sector
- Average industry turnover of 35% (according to Skills for Care)
- High demand for services due to increase in clients needing care
- Impact of Brexit on the labour market and availability of staff
- Increasing choice and opportunities for talented staff looking for a job
- Inability to meet Sustainable Transformation Plan Targets impacting on budgets
- Recruitment agents actively headhunting your existing staff
- Increase in safeguarding alerts caused by inconsistency in care delivery due to a lack of staff and temporary agency cover
- Aggressive recruitment from competitors in the market
- Competitors offering better value in terms of pay, benefits or career progression

Before & After: The Job Search In The Digital age

Have you ever watched 'Call the Midwife' and wondered how those nurses discovered a new job if they fancied a different challenge, career progression or change of scenery - without the help of Google or Facebook? It's highly likely that they relied on recommendations from family, friends or colleagues. They may have checked out the adverts in the local post office, newspaper, newsagent or asked in one of the recruitment agencies. Their choices were quite limited compared to the vast array of online -and offline- platforms available now to market and advertise your vacancy. In a lot of ways this is great news. You have the option of advertising offline in the post office, local newspapers, newsagents, leisure centres, job centre, universities, stall in the town centre…the list goes on. This is before you place ads online on specialised search engines like Indeed.com or StaffNurse.com, your website, own Facebook page, Twitter, Instagram, YouTube or LinkedIn - all without spending a lot of cash.

Many employers have discovered the added advantage of researching their candidates in more detail by checking out their Social Media profiles and digital footprint. Unsurprisingly, any serious applicant will do exactly the same thing to gather the insights they need to decide whether or not you are right for them. Their first stop will almost always be your website once you have captured their interest with your advertisement. How often do you step out of your office and into the shoes of your applicant, go on your webpage and apply for a job?

Auditing Your Application Process

Goals:

- To test the quality of your application process online and identify areas for improvement
- To follow the applicant's journey from the job advert to your desk

How to go about it:

Step 1: Start with A Baseline Check

- How many online applications do you receive versus offline?
- Which platform generates the greatest number of application forms?
- How many applications on average do you receive directly from your website?
- How many applications are you looking to generate to fill one vacancy?

Step 2: Check your digital advertising platforms

Which advertising channels do you currently use?

- Google
- Your own website
- Indeed.com
- StaffNurse.com
- Twitter account
- Facebook page
- LinkedIn
- Online advertising via a recruitment agency

Exercise:

Step 1: Imagine you are a candidate looking for a Support Worker job in the locality you are based. Set the timer on a stop watch or your phone and start your job search on Google. Type "Support Worker jobs in....(insert your county/city). How many search results come up? Do your job vacancies come up and are they on the first page of the search engine?

Step 2: Type in the job vacancy and the name of your own organisation. Does your website come up as the first search results? What other articles or links do you see mentioning you and your brand? Do they reflect you in a positive or negative light?

Step 3: Go to the home page on your website. Do you like the images you see? Does it have a friendly, professional and warm feel to it? Do you have a video to engage visitors? Research shows that visitors only spend 59sec-2min on a website before moving on.

Step 4: Can you see information straight away about the client group, service specification and organisation?

Step 5: How long does it take you to find "Join our team"?

Step 6: Check if you have to give your e-mail address before you can access the job vacancies

Step 7: Check your job page. Does it have video or written testimonials of staff? Do they come across authentic and real?

Step 8: Can you search jobs by geographical area?

Step 9: Does the job vacancy have: hourly rates of pay, benefits, breakdown of the training package, offer to get in touch for an informal chat or visit? When you press the "Apply Now" button, does the form come up straight away? How long does it take you to complete the application form? Do you get a notification letting you know it has been received with an estimated response time?

Step 10: Does your website have a blog with Social Media share buttons and a subscription offer? Do you have your latest CQC report and links to news from your service?

Take notes of your impressions and observations. Note down what you like/dislike about competitors websites and use this to get inspiration, insights and new ideas for your own website.

Why Your Website Matters

Your website presents your service to the outside world. It acts as a shop window for clients, families, commissioners, existing and future staff alike. Regardless of how potential candidates start their job search, they will probably go to your website to find out more before they submit their application. I suspect your website is currently designed and managed by your

IT or marketing department without your input. Potential candidates will either be impressed with the content it has to offer and how easy it is to navigate through interesting content until they reach the vacancy page, or they might decide that time is too precious to be wasted with creating a log-in account just to get more information about the vacancies on offer. Participants in my coaching courses spend 12 minutes plus trying to set up a login just to get past the basic job search. No one goes through that kind of hassle when research shows that we only spend an average of two minutes on a site before we lose interest and move on.

Features of an engaging and informative website:

- Pictures of clients and staff from your service
- Engaging headlines above the different sections
- A link to your latest CQC report
- Easy–to-navigate drop down menus
- A search/job search button
- The link to the job page is clear and easy to find
- Video
- Realistic written or video testimonials featuring real members of staff
- The job page is still linked to your organisation and does not take you to a site with a different name/logo
- The vacancy section contains all essential information such as location, working hours, salary range, and specific information on what training will be provided
- The vacancy page still has pictures and testimonials matching to the relevant job
- The application section has all relevant information and is straight forward to complete
- Social Media sharing buttons on every page with a link to the latest news/tweets

Niche marketing

Your Goals:

- Choose a target audience to maximise the impact of your marketing and advertising campaigns
- Create an avatar of your ideal candidate to use in your marketing campaign
- Tailor your marketing communications to influence your target audience

Definition: "Niche marketing is concentrating all marketing efforts on a small but specific and well defined segment of the population. Niches do not 'exist' but are created by identifying needs, wants, and requirements that are being addressed poorly or not all by other firms, and developing …services to satisfy them"

BusinessDictionary.com

How to go about it:

Step 1: Make a wish list by reviewing your job description and person specification. Who are you really looking for? What personal qualities, values, experience and skills are absolutely essential?

Are you looking for inexperienced staff, who would stay truly committed to spending three years in work based apprenticeship training? Do you need people with pre-existing care experience looking to move up the career ladder?

Step 2: Where are the people you are looking for working now? Ex-BHS staff with customer service skills are likely to be registered with the job centre, most likely looking for either another job in retail or opportunities to change direction. Experienced care staff will be employed by your competitors in the area.

How much time and money would staff be willing to spend to get to your workplace based on their future salary and current lifestyle?

Step 3: Focus on what your service has to offer. If you are working with clients who challenge, you may be able to offer staff the opportunity to develop their own specialist skill sets through working with them and additional training. How will this support their career choices in the future?

Step 4: Consider your service specifications and results for staff: Staff working in the Intellectual Disabilities Nursing and Care sector tend to have preferences of working with specific client groups such as autism, dual diagnosis, personality disorders, complex health needs, community based, forensic setting, etc. Is your setting slow paced or fast? Do clients stay short or long term ? If clients stay short term, staff will be able to observe progress quickly. If your service is longer, it gives staff unique opportunities to get to know the clients in-depth before they take the next steps on their care pathway.

Step 5: Synthesise all your ideas with the needs of your applicant. Tailor your advertising and marketing communication to include positive results, benefits and outcomes for your future workforce as well as clients. Balancing work with the demands of daily life has become a hot topic in recent years. What do you do to support healthy lifestyle choices? How is this reflected in your advertising and marketing communications?

Step 6: Now that you have identified your target audience and market, consider your advertising channels. Is the person you are looking for spending more time on Twitter or Facebook? Are they likely to use LinkedIn or Indeed.com for their job search? How will they see your advertisement?

How To Create An Avatar Of your Ideal Candidate

Imagine you want to attract the attention of ex-BHS staff, with a series of articles to build a relationship and help you fill your care vacancies further down the line.

Create a personal profile by putting yourself in the shoes of ex-BHS staff. It's often easier to think of a group of people as just one person. Let's say his name is Bill.

- What problems is Bill currently facing?

  Examples: he needs a job to pay the bills, there is a lot of competition for the jobs he is qualified for, he has a large family depending on him, he wants to stay in the local area, he is feeling anxious as he has been working for the same company for the past 20 years and has never applied for a new job in all that time, he is unsure whether to stay in retail or start over in a completely different field.

- What goals does Bill have?

  Examples: he is looking for a job close to home, he needs a job quickly, he wants to feel safe and secure, he is looking for stability for him and his family.

- What skills, experience and expertise does Bill have?

  Examples: customer-service experience, working under pressure, coping with shifts, mentoring colleagues, flexible, friendly, thriving in an ever-changing retail environment, taking on high levels of accountability and responsibility, loyal, etc.

Marketing Secrets

"What is the real value of your service for your clients?" I looked up at my coach with impatience and frustration. We had been going round and round in circles for quite some time now with my coach challenging me to come up with a solid response. I had spent hours carefully writing adverts, organising website content and researching how to spread the word about my service without breaking the bank. I was starting to regret even asking for some honest feedback on my marketing plans. Little did I know that my business would be completely transformed once I found the answer and unlocked the secrets of effective marketing.

The essence of marketing

Did you know that we are bombarded with an average of 2,500 adverts per day? This number was captured by following a person through a normal day, from getting up in the morning to going to bed. It is easy to conclude that marketing is all about advertising when we are confronted with that level of unrequested information on a daily basis. Many of us have learned to fight back and turn over television or radio channels as soon as any adverts come on. Marketers all over the world are scratching their heads, wondering how they can capture even a glimpse of our attention in the fast-paced, digital age. Industry gurus like Seth Godin or Brendon Burchard are encouraging businesses all over the world to spread their message by returning to the very essence of marketing, which is not about advertising and all about adding value instead.

The American Marketing Association defines marketing as 'the activity and processes for creating, communicating, delivering, and exchanging offerings that have value for customers, clients, partners, and society at large'. In a nutshell, your whole marketing strategy will become a whole lot more effective if you can add value to your future workforce and align all your communication with their current needs, goals, challenges and desires.

How to do marketing when you hate advertising

I have a confession to make: I hate advertising so much, I record the programs on the television just so that I can skip the adverts. When I opened my business, everyone was telling me that marketing is the one thing that will take me from zero to hero. After all, how could you possibly sell a service if no one knows of your existence?

I had full confidence in my ability to turn "The Coaching Nurse" from small start-up to a thriving enterprise. How hard could it possibly be with experience of coaching hundreds of people on their career journeys, a Diploma in Management Studies and formal teaching qualifications under my belt? A nosedive into all aspects of my business produced somewhat terrifying results. Sales figures produced a big fat zero. My marketing budget had dwindled to £100. My bank balance was running the risk of tipping into red figures. I decided over breakfast one morning that I would close up shop for good if I could not find one paying customer within ninety days. Not ready to throw in the towel just yet, I started to researched thought leaders of our time and applied their advice to my business. I learned from expert marketers that your advert makes precious little impact, when a research study shows we see an average of 2,500 advertisements in one day alone. Reading the classic 'How to win friends and influence people' by Dale Carnegie led me to a complete lightbulb moment. I stopped bothering busy professionals with advertisements and flyers. I chose to invest some time in getting to really know people and their problems before sharing possible solutions across online -and offlinc- platforms. This new approach transformed my business and led to clients contacting me instead of the other way around.

CHAPTER FOUR

How To Engage your future workforce

Promoting Your Service In The Digital Age

How would you like a strategy that involves your current workforce in your recruitment plans, creates a candidate pipeline, expands your influence, supports profits and positions you ahead of the competition? Thought so! I will show you a clear process you can follow to achieve all of these goals in addition to improving the effectiveness of your current marketing communications. I want to introduce you to content-marketing, which is commonly defined as relationship-based marketing. "How to win friends and influence people" remains one of the cult business books with millions of copies sold worldwide. In it, Dale Carnegie advocates that to really get to know a person and build trust and influence, offer something of value first. Content-marketing is based on exactly the same concept and has become the chosen marketing method of thought leaders around the globe. If you have ever read a blog, learned something new in a workshop or watched a YouTube video to get a quick piece of advice, you will have experienced and taken full advantage of this powerful system.

Quick Start Your Content Marketing Strategy

Your goals:

- Create a contact database or pipeline of interested candidates
- Engage your existing workforce into your recruitment strategies, making it more effective
- Compliment your existing digital media marketing strategy
- Tangible measures and metric of your influence
- Expand your online and offline networks
- Improve your ratings on internet search engines such as Google, Facebook and YouTube
- Create a unique selling point and differentiate you from other employers on the market
- Build organisational memory

Definition: "Content marketing is the marketing and business process for creating and distributing relevant and valuable content to attract, acquire, and engage a clearly defined and understood target audience-with the objective of driving profitable customer action" — contentmarketinginstitute.com

How to go about it:

Step 1: Decide your goals and outcomes

Do you want to expand your network? Increase your influence? Build a contact base? Help your existing workforce meet their reflective practice goals and set yourself apart from the competition? Be able to connect with potential candidates way before you ask them to fill in an application form, on as many platforms as possible?

Step 2: Consider how you will measure your results.

The number of blog subscribers will automatically increase your contact database. The 'like' and 'share' buttons on Social Media will tempt you into judging your work by the number of people liking and sharing your content. How many staff are happy to write an article for your blog or give a short presentation? Once published, they will want to share their creative composition with family and friends.

Step 3: Create an avatar for your target audience

Who will be reading or watching your content? The interest of people will only be sparked with content that is relevant and helpful to them. Create an avatar of your readership by thinking about the current issues, goals and challenges your audience is facing at this moment in time. How can your blog give them what they want? What results are they really looking for? What problems are they trying to solve?

Step 4: Brainstorm

Use all the information you have so far to brainstorm as many topics as possible for future features and content. Here are some examples to get you started:

- From retail to care: why choosing care was the best decision ever
- How to fill in an application forms in 3 simple steps
- Transferrable skills: How your expertise can change someone's life
- 5 things to consider when on a career crossroads
- 5 tips to nail any interview
- 3 things you didn't know about recruitment days

Step 5: Structure your article

- Decide on a catchy headline

    The headline will get people excited about your article. Consider the headlines you click on or want to know more about. If you get stuck, just google: Jon Morrow, headline hacks. It will give you a free template of headlines you can use and adapt.

- Write a short summary of what the article is all about and what the reader will learn

  Example: Application forms can seem really daunting if you haven't filled one out in a long time. This article will give you three helpful tips how to get it done and give you a really good chance of nailing that all important interview.

- Follow this with your tips

- Call to action: Write a sentence to close and include a contact link for people to find out more or get in touch. Ensure you encourage your readers to share the article. You can also include a link to your job vacancies.

- Always include at least one image in your article.

- Publish your article

Step 6: Publish your content

This is probably the most important step after writing it. Sharing your content on different online platforms such as your own website, Twitter, Linkedin, your Facebook page, internal e-mail system will ensure it reaches your audience far and wide. You only need to take a look at your own Social Media news feeds to get an idea how many posts fight for your attention in the fast -paced cyber space. Successful content marketeers overcome this obstacle by carefully selecting only the platforms frequented by their audience as well as posting their content multiple times throughout the day.

Alternatively, you could contact Community of Practice groups running their own blog and check if it would be possible to submit an article as a guest author.

What If People Don't Like My Stuff?

When I started my own blog, I would often feel a wave of relief wash over me mixed with my heart pounding in nervous excitement. Would my readers find the article helpful? What if someone read it and didn't like it or worse, no one liked it on Facebook or watched it on YouTube? It took me a little while to learn that even the most successful bloggers with millions of followers count their lucky stars if their work gets noticed by a handful of people. Every book on blogging or content marketing advocates two vital ingredients for success: the commitment to produce your blog and the confidence to keep going no matter how many followers you have or how many likes you get. Things really turned around for me one day when I read this sentence in a book "All knowledge is wasted if it stays in your head!" This made a lot of sense to me and just thinking of how many people may get a new idea or insight from my work keeps me on track each week. Taking this approach allows me to share my expertise in the knowledge it will be accessible and available to future generations of HR -and healthcare professionals in years to come

What Makes People Tick?

Your goal: To understand the underlying psychology of marketing and sales

How to go about it:

Knowing what drives our purchasing decisions is the Holy Grail for many marketers. This is the real reason your peaceful evening is disturbed by cold callers on the search for vital clues, helping them to inform their next advertising campaign. One man decided to fight back. Dr. Robert Cialdini went on a quest to uncover the hidden strategies used by sales -and marketing professionals. His book "Influence: The Psychology of Persuasion" identifies the following key weapons:

1. Reciprocation: You give something…and take something
2. Commitment and Consistency
3. Social Proof/Testimonials
4. Likeability
5. Authority
6. Scarcity

You can see all of them in action in daily life. Here are just some examples:

1.) **Reciprocation**: Sticky notes, pens, chocolates…you can find all of these items at most conference stands all over the country. Of course, picking them up is really helpful when replenishing your stationary supplies. It's good to know though that there is a natural desire inside of us to give back and return the favour.

2.) **Commitment and Consistency**: Have you ever had any recruitment agent on the phone asking you if your day is going well and you said yes? Did you find yourself say yes to the next question, which probably was a request to send some CV's over? This is no coincidence. Once we commit ourselves to yes, we tend to feel the need to be consistent in our responses. This leads to us saying yes when we really would prefer to say no.

3.) **Social Proof/Testimonials**: Do your kids ever come to you asking for the latest game or trainers because all their friends are raving about it? Did you ever find yourself getting interested in a book or movie after your friend gave it a glowing review? We often lack the time or capacity to research the best deals and make an informed choice. On the whole, we have stopped trusting brand advertising. We have a lot more confidence in recommendations from families, friends or peers.

4.) **Likeability**: Have you ever had a friend invite you to a Tupperware or candle party? At the end of the night, did you find yourself placing orders even though you didn't really need a bowl that lasts forever or romantic lighting? It should come as no surprise that we are more likely to buy from people we like!

5.) **Authority**: A psychologist carrying out a research study once paid students to put on a white coat, go into a busy post office, shout "Let me through, I'm a doctor" and jump the queue. 90% of people gave way. When the experiment was repeated, only 10% of people gave up their space in line. The only difference? There was no white coat the second time around. The same thing happens in advertising. TV commercials featuring a testimonial from a doctor or expert get a greater response compared to adverts simply featuring the product.

Building A Candidate Pipeline

Having the ability to build a contact list and pipeline of prospects is the key advantage of publishing regular blogs or videos. Every blog subscriber could be a potential candidate or may know someone, who is looking for a job in healthcare. It gives you the opportunity to interact with your audience, find out more about their current situation and respond with helpful hints and tips. Once you have a system in place to develop and share content, you will be able to use it for online and offline networking. Imagine you show up at a recruitment fair. All of your competitors talk to people and hand out standard application packs. You on the other hand chat to people, offer them your latest article with the best tips to prepare for interview in addition to your own recruitment pack. When the person gets home, they will empty their bag and only keep what's valuable to them. Say your potential prospect is actively looking for a job and decides to keep your tips and tricks on their desk. The piece of paper will become a frequent reminder of you and your job opportunity on offer.

Go to the free bonus chapter for more ideas on how to get the most out of your networking opportunities: http://thecoachingnurse.org.uk/fill-50-jobs-in-90-days-bonus-chapter/

Why Your Workforce Is Your Secret Weapon

What is the one thing you crave more than anything else when you come to work? Of course, the answer will vary, depending on your reason for taking your job in the first place. Working in challenging healthcare environments for the majority of my career has made me realised that there is one thing your workforce desires more than money, status or promotion: safety.

Coming on shift, you want to be a hundred percent sure that the person next to you knows the care plans, risk assessments and clients as well as you do. Being able to rely on your colleague when things fall apart is a vital feature of any team. No matter what challenges the shift throws at you, you can get through anything with trusted colleagues at your side.

You don't want to walk in your office only to be greeted with new work colleagues every single day and neither does your workforce. The difference between you and them? It happens to them every single time an inexperienced member of agency becomes part of their crew for the day.

Throw all of these factors together and it's easy to see why your workforce have a vast personal interest in sorting out recruitment and retention problems.

There may have been a time when marketing was the sole job of the marketing department, with support from Senior Managers. Not anymore! Abuse in care homes hits the news on a frequent basis. This means that the general population has become more suspicious of what goes on behind closed doors. Your staff are in the best position to market your jobs and shine a bright light on your service.

Any Support Workers taking the plunge from a different industry into care will know the doubts they faced during their first month in the job and can share how they successfully settled into their new occupation. Experienced staff can provide much needed advice, how to go from surviving to thriving when working with different client groups. Qualified staff nurses could write down their take on successful shift leading to support their continuous professional development and meet re-validation requirements.

CHAPTER FIVE

Assess your candidate

The Best Method To Assess Application Forms

Has the candidate…

….previous experience in care? Yes

…..QCF/NVQ level 2 training? Yes

…Completed all sections of the form including supporting information?

Looking at the twelve-page handwritten life-history that my candidate, (let's call him Bob) attached to his form, I determined that yes, supportive information was definitely provided. I should have been elated. A candidate with everything I was looking for and more. Unfortunately, Bob's biography did not tell me what brought him to care in the first place, whether or not he was enjoying it or why he was applying for this particular job at all. Alarm bells started to ring loudly when I arrived on page eight, which contained a variety of criminal cautions and convictions. A count-up of points and a deep sigh and Bob's application had made its way firmly into my 'No' pile.

After assessing the rest of my application forms, I was left with 20 rejections and 15 applicants about to be invited to the upcoming recruitment day. Out of these 15, 10 people showed up on the day. After interviews and practical assessment tests, seven candidates were offered a position with 5 staying longer than 12 months.

When my colleague from HR first introduced the idea of developing a short assessment form with a scoring system to measure the suitability of applicants more objectively, I was doubtful. It kind of reminded me of a test you would find in Cosmo magazine. When I analysed our recruitment situation six months later, I noticed that the recruitment -as well as retention rates had significantly improved. I was also able to provide a clear rationale for accepting or rejecting applicants.

How Choosy Should You Be?

What started out with a plain letter inviting you to an interview for your dream job has somehow become the stuff of nightmares. The stack of problems you are about to face seems as high as the mountain you and 199 other candidates are clinging to in the desperate hope of landing the job.

The pouring rain drenches your clothes together with your backpack. What was once a small footpath right on the edge of the cliff has morphed into one long mudslide. The sound of raindrops fail to drone out the unruly voice in your head torn between the desire to reach your goal and the temptation to stop right there and then. You have worked too hard for this to give up now. Relief coupled with fear washes over you when you see the end is near. Crossing the finish line will mean either total failure to pass selection or complete victory in becoming part of the elite and starting your induction training with the SAS.

"Many try to get into the Special Air Services regiment. Most of them fail. Out of an average intake of 125 candidates, the gruelling selection process will weed out all but 10." www.eliteukforces.info/special-air-service/sas-selection/

The different stages of the recruitment tests both mental and physical capabilities of candidates. Only the very best succeed in securing themselves a place in this elite organisation. When was the last time you heard someone in the care sector say that their number of suitable applicants for a vacancy far outweighs the number of vacancies every year? Exactly. It just doesn't happen, despite the fact that working in this sector gives as well as demands a highly specialised skills set. Ask anyone in the sector what they see as the biggest threat to their service and I guarantee the clinical, regulatory or economic consequences of offering the job to the wrong person will be high on the list. I want to share with you the tried and tested strategies I used to choose the right people in the first place and thereby reducing the risks to the service.

How To Organise Recruitment Days

What comes after the application form for you? It's likely that you will either invite your candidate for interviews, possibly with a tour around your place or more comprehensive recruitment days with presentations, a tour round, interviews and activities involving the clients and existing staff.

Organising whole recruitment days or assessment centres can seem a bit excessive when you have a lot of work on and you are pressured to hit your financial targets. On the other hand, you could save a small fortune if you can link all of your recruitment activities with the goal of increasing the number of people successfully staying with you through induction and beyond.

Recruitment days turned into a real asset for me when I noticed that candidates relished the chance of getting to know their future workplace, colleagues and clients in more depth. Existing staff readily volunteered to take the lead on specific activities. Clients valued that they had a real say into who would be supporting them on their care pathway in the months to come. Undeniably, the most important benefit was the dramatic increase in staff retention rates following the introduction of recruitment days.

1.) Decide on the basic components of the day. This may be registration and coffee, presentation, activities such as case studies with team discussion, supported activities with clients, interview, a tour round and finally an evaluation of the day.

2.) Risk assess everything! It doesn't matter what client group you have or the setting you are operating in; your risk assessment for the day has to be done!

3.) Find willing helpers from your staff team and if possible different departments. A loyal member of staff sharing all the reasons they enjoy working for you can greatly influence your candidate's choices. Offering a short overview of a typical day will allow your candidate to picture themselves already doing the job and having a good time.

4.) Decide on the key goal of your presentations. Every speech is designed to move people towards taking action. Be clear what you want candidates to feel and do once they've listened to your talk. Since public speaking is an integral element of recruitment, I have explored the topic in more depth in Chapter 6.

5.) Use real-life problems as the starting point for planning real-life scenario activities, interviews or case studies. This will give your candidate a good understanding of what is expected of them and help them make an informed choice.

6.) Don't forget to include regular breaks and encourage participants to ask questions throughout the day

7.) A tour around the place is the perfect way to showcase everything that is good about your place, build rapport and get to know your candidate in a more relaxed setting. It is also a great opportunity for your staff to tell their stories for maximum influence. Storytelling is a great way of connecting with people quickly. I have included the best strategies and exercises how you can build your own story in Chapter 6.

8.) Research options to include the clients you care for. This might be paying them with vouchers to participate in interviews asking their own pre-agreed questions or organising short group activities. If possible, capture their feedback with short evaluation forms.

9.) Talking of feedback -and evaluation forms; don't forget to find out from your candidates what they have really enjoyed about the day and suggestions for future recruitment days.

10.) Involve the staff leading the different activities throughout the day in your final decision-making process. Saying yes or no will not always be straight forward. You might find yourself in a situation, where you consider compromising, giving people a chance or having to reject seemingly good candidates after evaluating feedback from everyone. Making the right decision is crucial to your future business success. The next section will show you how you can choose with confidence and reduce the risk to your service.

Is This Person Worth The Risk?

"He was a bit quiet in the team-building task and he didn't get that many questions right at interview, but he was really nervous. He was excellent with the clients though and he seems such a nice guy. I think we should give him a chance. I reckon with a bit of mentoring he will be alright!"
After my colleagues passionate pitch on the end of long recruitment day, Barry's* file lands firmly on the 'yes' pile.
I am full of regrets just eight weeks later. Barry has managed to break a chair during induction training, gets easily distracted and doesn't seem to respond to mentoring. When I tell my colleagues I have made a decision to end Barry's probation and our misery early, my colleagues tell me that he probably just needs a little more time to adjust and they will help him find his feet. Pushing my lingering doubts aside, I agree for him to stay. In the month that follows, Barry's attendance rates drops and he is antagonising staff and clients alike by not following care plans or risk assessments. With a heavy heart I choose to fail his End of Probation and let him go. Going through this experience made me realise that I have to evaluate opportunities carefully before reaching a decision.
*Name changed to protect privacy

When is it worth taking a risk? How do you know when to say no to an opportunity and walk away? Research from the Oxford Institute of Economics predicts an estimated cost of £30,000 to replace just one employee. Just think of how much cash, not to mention time and effort you could save if you could find a way to get it right more often than not.

Before I show you how some of the top coaches in the world recommend you do this, let's take another look at Barry's case and explore some of the questions you could have asked before you decided on yes or no:

- How much mentoring is "a bit of mentoring' exactly?
- What specifically are you looking to teach your candidate in addition to induction?
- Who is the best person to provide this training and how long would this take?
- Who would be missing out if you provide additional support?
- What option produces the least amount of work? Extra mentoring or the search for another applicant?
- Have you had this situation in the past? How did you deal with it? What was the end result?

Opportunity evaluator

How to evaluate opportunities in 4 steps

Brendon Burchard is one of the most successful performance coaches in the industry. He recommends assessing the level of time, support and ownership to help you determine if something is a good opportunity or not. You can find Brendon's opportunity evaluator here:
https://www.youtube.com/watch?v=QrIet-MuueQ

I have used his model as a baseline for this quick step-by step process you can use when confronted with though recruitment decisions:

Step 1: Who owns or is responsible for this problem or need? You might think if you are in charge of recruitment, it's definitely you. On the other hand, the responsibility to train and mentor a candidate may be with your colleagues from the training department. The ownership for meeting your expected standards at the beginning lies with your candidates.

Step 2: Determine the level of resources required to mentor this person. Who will miss out and not benefit from your support during this time?

Step 3: Consider what would really help this person the most and consider if you are really able and willing to provide all the necessary resources this person requires.

Step 4: Involve your team in this process. A review of all current needs and future implications will give you confidence in your choices.

If The Plant In Your Office Could Talk..

If the plant in your office could talk, what would it say about your organisational skills?

When was the last time you've quizzed your applicant and threw them with a surprising interview question? There is nothing worse than sitting in interviews asking the same old questions and getting the same old predictable answers in return.

The interview is often the last hurdle standing between your candidate and a job offer. There was a time people got really nervous about interviews. They had no idea what questions might come their way. Nowadays, all you need to do is order a book from Amazon, prepare and practice your own responses, and e voila, you've bagged yourself a new career!

Why not mix it up a little? I have put together a new take on the most popular interview questions here:

Ask this: If I would ask your best friend about your personal qualities, what would he or she say?
Not that: What are your strengths and weaknesses?

Ask this: Think about a time you have failed to achieve a goal. What positive feedback did you take away from this?
Not that: How do you cope with failures?

Ask this: Imagine we offer you the job and we meet again in a month's time. What aspects of the role would you enjoy the most? What could you do without?
Not that: Why do you want this job?

Ask this: Imagine your strategies to achieve a goal have all failed. What would you do to get new ideas?
Not that: Tell me about a time you were faced with a challenge. What did you do?

Ask this: Why are challenging clients/colleagues good for you?
Not that: How do you cope with challenging clients/colleagues?

Ask this: Say I would want to see how you cope when you are absolutely stressed to the hilt. What would need to happen to get you to that point?
Not that: How do you cope with stress?

Ask this: Imagine this job could take you anywhere at all. Where would you really want to go? What do you want to experience?
Not that: Where do you want to be in five years' time?

When picking the wrong team burns £250m

Many professionals working in Intellectual Disabilities Nursing -and Care today will cite Winterbourne View as a terrifying example of what happens when the fate of clients without a voice is left in the hands of criminals. The unfortunate fact of the matter is that at one point in time the very same people appearing in court charged with neglect and assault to name just a few, were deemed suitable for the job. Winterbourne View is an uncomfortable lesson for clinicians, accountants, HR professionals, CEOs and investors alike. After all, if someone had told you that 20 staff could bring down a leading brand in the sector with an estimated financial worth of £250m, would you really believe them?

Imagine its 2006 and you are the new Chief Executive of one of the leading healthcare specialists providing services to people with Learning Disabilities. Your company is very valuable. You have taken the job after a deal worth a cool £255m. The years go by and business is booming. Local authorities pay you around £3,500 per week per patient. Just one unit of your extensive portfolio stretching across 20+ units rakes in £4m a year. Even the regulators seem to love you. The CQC gives you good scores on the doors.

Let's fast forward to May 2011. You have had a hectic day. You decide to chill out watching a bit of telly. Panorama is just starting. Suddenly time seems at a standstill. You recognise the pictures on the screen. The unit. The corridors. The lounge. The Garden. It looked quite idyllic when you walked through them. Now they are filled with staff flinging patients around. Subjecting them to horrific abuse. You want to make it stop as your heart is pounding faster. Waves of panic wash over you as you watch patients having mouthwash poured into their eyes. Being held down with great force as medication is forced into their mouth. Listening to the former Staff Nurse explain how all his complaints fell onto death ears with management. It is the day that not just your life changes forever. It is also the day that care for people with Intellectual Disabilities will never be the same again.

'Winterbourne View' has become a synonym for horrific abuse targeting the most vulnerable members of our society. 19 complaints had already been raised by staff members inside the home internally as well as externally before Panorama started filming. 6 out of 11 care staff were jailed with charges over abuse, ill treatment and neglect. Everyone asking the same question: How could this been allowed to happen?

Castlebeck, the operator of Winterbourne View put a large amount of work into transforming their services. However, the organisation never survived the scandal. Castlebeck went into administration just two years after the Panorama programme.

The group of former staff members participating in the abuse have done a lot more than close down a residential hospital and destroy the value of the Castlebeck brand. The fall-out, investigations and actions plans from Winterbourne View have changed the landscape of Learning Disability Nursing & Care forever.

The government vowed to move people with Learning Disabilities from residential hospitals into smaller community settings. The Care Quality Commission has pledged to change the way they inspect services in response to their own failings. Safeguarding teams have become extra vigilant when investigating incidents. The issue of consistent training addressed, by asking staff just beginning to complete the care certificate.

As with every disaster it is not all doom and gloom. Some providers clearly have spotted the business opportunity for small, high quality care services in the community. The case of Winterbourne View demonstrates like no other how poor recruitment decisions can destroy a once lucrative and valuable business. If you have read or heard of the government initiative 'Transforming Care', you will know that the implications and consequences of Winterbourne View for any provider in this sector are far from over.

CHAPTER SIX
How To Negotiate With Your Candidate

Do you pay sticker price?

Have you ever been on the way to a car dealership feeling absolutely certain that you were going to spend a set amount and not a penny more?

I always remember the day I went car shopping with my Dad. Arriving back at the dealership after test driving a brand new Suzuki Swift I had fallen in love with, he got out and left. We tried out four other cars before we were back. I was still starring longingly at the car when I overheard the following conversation between my Dad and George, the sales man:

"We like the car, but £18,000 is too steep. I'm only a farmer. I really can't afford that much"

George promptly went down to £17,500. My dad shook his head, talked about the bad harvest it has been and said that he could pay cash, but could only pay £16,000 absolute maximum. After some back and forth, George agreed and said we could pick up the car on Thursday. "With a full tank of petrol?" George shook his head smiling before confirming that yes, there would be petrol. My dad managed to persuade George to include some foot mats and a First Aid box so the deal was done.

The whole experience taught me everything you really need to know about negotiating. I learned that there tends to be wiggle room when you purchase big ticket items. Considering your annual salary, jobs do fall into that category. You can get a good deal if you can offer value and you are clear about your desired outcome. Building rapport is just as important as knowing how far you are willing to go. Everyone wants to feel a winner when closing the deal.

Here are my top tips for interview negotiations:

1. Give people a reason to stay

It's natural for you to want good people, who will stay for all eternity. How likely is that really going to happen? People do move on and you will put yourself in a much better position when you consider, from the beginning, how long you want people to stay. Setting a timeframe for staff retention will allow you to analyse the real value of your vacancy to your employees. How do you support their personal -and professional goals during this time? How will working for you change them as a person? What lifestyle will become affordable once people take the job, now and in the future?

2. Can your candidate deliver?

How badly do you need someone? I remember a time when a former employee wanted to return to work for us. He demanded to return at the top end of the salary band; explaining that he had gained a lot of experience whilst he was away. When I compared his demand with the wages of existing staff, I discovered that there were only three people in that wage bracket. Imagining a potential fall out within the team in addition to not knowing if the person could really deliver, I said no. Even though I was desperate, the risk was just too high for me.

Is there a pattern of your candidate hopping from job to job every two years? If so, what makes you think this would be any different in your place? Once you know that this is a real risk, you can weigh up if it's worth the cost of recruiting and training someone in exchange for having someone in post for 24 months.

3. What is really on the table?

- Make a list of everything you can give in addition to hard cash.
- Your list may include your flexible working policy, free training courses, mentoring for career progression, apprenticeship schemes, opportunities to engage in research, a chance to spend time with colleagues in other departments, presenting at external conferences and events, developing a specialist skill, etc.

4. What does your candidate really want?

Put yourself in the shoes of your candidate. What are they really after? Hard cash or recognition?

Internal staff surveys will often show staff feeling overworked and underpaid. In other words, they can't see that their contribution is valued. Everyone wants to make a good impression with a new employer; this means nobody ever tells you this in so many words. You can overcome this obstacle and build credibility by giving candidates the option of meeting current employees.

5. How far would you go?

This lesson always served me well when I ended up in salary negotiations with candidates. I never used to ask potential employees how much they wanted to earn, until I had to use recruitment agencies to source qualified applicants. With a tour round, presentation and interview all going really well, we would decide to offer the position. That was when the trouble started. The agent almost always called me back after relaying the happy news back to their candidate to let me know that their candidate loves the place, but doesn't like the number on the table. Many recruitment agencies charge a percentage fee of the starting salary. Trying to get a better deal benefits them as much as their candidate. Once I realised this, I turned the tables.

Once applicants had asked all of their questions, I would enquire what salary they would be happy with. Not many people responded with figures. Only a handful of applicants went through the trouble of explaining why they thought they were worth that much.

There is still the myth around that you are in a better position if you can pay £1 more. Having seen some colleagues leave for jobs that paid way below their existing wage, I really doubt that this is true. Of course, cash will always be king for some people. What really matters to you when you choose a job? I am willing to bet that it's not money alone. Research by Forbes has shown that learning and being happy tops earning potential. Having a sense of purpose came in fourth place. I believe it may rank higher for employees in the caring profession. Knowing what really matters to the other person will always give you a key advantage during any type of negotiations, whether it's at home or at work.

What Everyone Wants And No One Offers

"What do I need to do to get that job?"

My boss looked at me surprised. My colleague was leaving and I had turned up with a very clear agenda.

I wanted to find out as much as possible about expectations, requirements and pitfalls from someone who had done the job in the past. Once home, I took out my notes, checked off the skills I already had and made a plan to gain the qualifications I would need. I wrote down possible obstacles together with a plan on how I would overcome them. I suddenly had a real career strategy, thanks to my boss giving me insider information.

How many employers currently offer free career clinics and advise to their employees? Not that many.

How often do you hear anyone share their own career journey including the times they stumbled and got back up? Unless someone specifically asked for it, probably never. I believe this is a big oversight. Giving future employees a jump start up the career ladder could secure you a signature on the dotted line in addition to trust, respect and loyalty in years to come.

Win People Over With Your Presentation

Did you know that public speaking is ranked as the number 1 fear by most people regardless of education, background or status? It's right up there together with snakes, spiders or crocodiles. It is good to know that all fears are learned fears and we are not born with them. Many artists performing in front of large crowds as part of their job will tell you that to this day they still feel butterflies just before they go on stage. Olympian Mo Farah says the rush of adrenaline propels him over the finish line when the going gets though.

Many of you will have "the ability to engage the workforce in change through positive communications" as part of your job description. In a nutshell, this means you need to be able to move people from A to B with the power of your talk. How hard can it be? The truth is: very! There is a reason politicians practice word patterns, use professional writers and spend time researching their audience. They are very aware that every speech has a job to to.
Speakers throughout history have been able to influence and challenge our thinking with the power of their words. Even short snippets make them instantly recognisable to this day:

"I have a dream" -Martin Luther King Jr.
"We will fight them on the beaches" Winston Churchill

I believe some of the fear of public speaking comes from the fact that we are not sure how we can follow in the footsteps of greatness. I like to think of it in a slightly different way. Why not 'stand on the shoulders of giants' as Anthony Robbins would say by following their recipe for success?

I found one of the most helpful plan for creating a persuasive talk in Brian Tracy's book "The 6 Figure Speaker.." He recommends using the following roadmap for any presentation:

Step 1: Care about your topic. It's true that there may well be times you will have to speak on topic you can't get excited about. If this happens, consider how the message of your talk will benefit your audience.

Step 2: Consider the length of your talk. The shorter your timeframe, the harder it is to fit your message into the given timeframe. Check out first how long you have and what you really want your audience to take away.

Step 3: Watch or listen to some TED talks or search Youtube. You will find that there is something to be learned from everyone. Having watched Daniel H. Pink's funny talk on what really motivates us, I discovered how to get maximum impact from very sparingly used PowerPoint slides. If you are an avid fan of TV shows such as 'Scandal' or 'Grey's Anatomy', you probably enjoy writer Shonda Rhimes moving the audience to tears of laughter!

Step 4: Research as much as possible about your audience and define your intended goal or outcome. What are they interested in? What do you want to happen or what do you want people to do as a consequence of your talk?

Step 5: Write your key points, ideas, and phrases on index cards and use them to jog your memory during your talk or presentation

Step 6: Visualise your talk over and over again. Imagine yourself in front of people, who have your best interest at heart. They are supportive and on your side. Many of us have no trouble hitting the play button on the horror scenario where everything is falling apart. You wouldn't go to the cinema and watch the same terrible horror film again and again. It's time to hit the stop button and change the movie. Create a story of confidence and competence and play that as many times as you want. Do you remember Jonny Wilkinson kicking the winning goal in the last minutes of the Rugby World cup in 2003? When asked about his performance, Wilkinson named visualisation as one of his key strategies for success.

Step 7: Structure your speech in the following way:

- Tell the audience what you are going to tell them and what they will learn
- State your opinion on a particular topic and the reasons for your point of view
- Back this up with an example, easy to digest statistics or a short case study story
- Re-iterate your point of view and repeat this structure for all of your points

Here are some of the most helpful Do's and Don't's I picked up during my research into public speaking skills:

Do:

- Consider starting with a story to engage your audience
- Tell your audience what they will get out of your talk right away
- Round up your talk by summarising your key points and give your audience action points
- Break down statistics in easy to understand numbers. For instance: say 4 out of 10 instead of 40%
- Use your voice to re-iterate important messages
- Practice different ways to communicate the core of your message
- Mix up your talk by including quotes, stories and relevant statistics

Don't

- Use PowerPoint when it's not necessary. We all heart the phrase 'Death by PowerPoint"
- Fill your PowerPoint slides with lots and lots of writing. Use pictures instead to compliment your points
- Rush through your talk. Practice slowing down your words -and sentences
- Let fear prevent you from showing up in the first place

How to Pitch With A Story

Have you ever made friends real quick by telling them a good story? Throughout centuries, people have used this technique to share their knowledge and pass on their expertise to the next generation. Famous speakers have been able to alter the course of history with the power of their stories. Most of us grow up with fairy tales; and whether it's Star Wars or Scandal, we all find ourselves drawn into a gripping plot.

Think of your favourite movie for a second. What happens?

Do you get to know your hero just before you go on a magical adventure full of surprises, fun and adventure? Does your hero practice, practice, practice before facing down ferocious enemies with the help of newfound friends? Has your hero turned into a completely different person by the time the film ends?

How is possible for me to guess how the story goes without knowing even the title of the film? I wish I could sell it to you as a little sparkle of magic. Not so. Joseph Campbell researched a multitude of stories for his book "The Hero with a thousand faces". He literally read thousands of stories and discovered most of them follow the same structure. Joseph Campbell uncovered a framework used by everyone from Hollywood producers to J.K.Rowling: the Hero's journey.

Plenty of organisations have recognised have seen the light, ditched the boring powerpoint and replaced it with stories of good fighting evil in the corporate world in the hope you will join their team. You only need to watch one episode of Dragon's Den to see how stories are a lot more effective when you want to move and influence your audience.

"The Hero's journey" story structure:

1. We are introduced to the hero of the story
2. Something happens, circumstances change and our hero is going on a journey
3. Our hero is facing a new challenge and initially fails to conquer the challenge
4. Our hero is learning new skills and finds a mentor
5. Our hero makes new friends along the way
6. Our hero battles with fear (often called 'the shadow')
7. Our hero is ready to face his enemy
8. Big battle
9. Our hero returns a changed person

How To Use It For Your Own Pitch:

Step 1: Think of a challenge you have successfully overcome

Step 2: Review the structure. Can you re-create your story to follow this structure?

Step 3: Create a repertoire of different stories. Any pitch, promotion or presentation will always be more interesting if you kick of with a story. Play your cards right and your story could become your secret weapon of influence. It is best to have a variety of stories, so you can choose one that relates to the circumstances of your audience.

Step 4: Remember to have a look around the websites of your competitors. If there are client case studies, check out if they follow 'The Hero's journey' and rate on a scale of 1-5 the quality of the story.

CHAPTER SEVEN
Staff Retention Strategies

Getting staff in the door is one thing, persuading them to stay quite another. This penultimate chapter offers suggestions, strategies and concepts to strengthen your staff retention and reduce turnover.

How To Make Supervision Count

How often do you hear people say they are "fine" and they are really "fine?" Exactly!

I remember the day I had my first supervision meeting. I was so excited. I had done the training, I was well prepared, I was ready....until my member of staff arrived. The form had quite a lot of questions covered everything from patient experience to working with colleagues. Unfortunately, my member of staff answered all questions with just one word "Fine".

This blog gives you coaching tools to use in your supervision sessions to helps you get past common barriers of communication. It offers you the tools to breakthrough and move forward.

1. "I've had enough. I don't always want to be the one picking up all the work"

Possible questions:

- What do you want instead?
- From what you are saying, it looks like you want to ensure work is shared out fairly?

2. "Nothing is going right. No matter what I do, there is just endless criticism"

Possible questions:

- Imagine you are in the cinema, watching a day at work like a movie. Can you pick up the moments where things are going the way you want them to be?
- What are they? Who is there with you? Make those pictures 3D and observe. What's different?

3. "Everything is fine"

Possible questions:

- If you could change one thing around here, what would it be?
- Imagine I would have asked you to write a note with three things you want to discuss today last night. What would the note say?

4. "I'm not going anywhere in this organisation. My skills are just wasted"

Possible questions:

- Get a piece of paper and a pen and draw a timeline starting from the date your member of staff joined the organisation. Mark the dates of completing induction, End of Probation, first ward round, first CPA meeting, first supervision meeting, first appraisal, any projects....ask the member of staff what other moments stand out for them and why. What skills have they used? What experience gained? Have they got other moments that really stood out for them? What was special?

- Move the line into the future. Ask your member of staff to put markers in with dates and what skills, knowledge and experience they would like to gain between now and then

5. "Nobody cares about the work we do. We've put everything into this project and now its scrapped thanks to budget cuts."

Possible questions:

- Ask your colleague about someone they really admire and just for a moment pretend this person is coming to visit to find out everything they can about this project. How did it start? What went really well? Highlights?
- What challenges did you face? How did you overcome them? If it was a story, what would need to happen to give it a happy ending?

When People Mess Up

It was Saturday afternoon around 3pm when it happened. Looking at a patient's drug card I saw that prescribed lunchtime medication had not been signed for. I gave it to the patient. As soon as the patient had swallowed the tablet, she said "Oh, I'm sure I had this tablet earlier!"
I phoned my colleague. She confirmed that she had given the medication but forgot to sign for it. I filled in the medication error form with a sinking heart. After a weekend of anxiety and worry, Monday morning finally came. I approached my manager and apologised for my error. I explained that I learned not to take things on face value. To check if I was not sure. To seek advice if things do go wrong. He looked at me and said "We all make

mistakes. Thank you for bringing it to my attention."

I once told this tale in a discussion round and someone asked "What would have happened if your boss would have not been this understanding?"

This question got me thinking about the internal motivators for covering up mistakes, what we might tell ourselves in addition to coaching techniques for personal development and growth.

#1 "People will think I am incompetent!"

Consider: How do you know? What evidence have you got to support this assumption? Who specifically? Your competence has grown over time. How? What have been real times of learning for you?

#2 "If I admit to this, I'm going to get in real trouble. I may go to disciplinary."

Consider: What was your main reason for becoming a nurse or a doctor? Let's say, it's helping people and saving lives. How does not saying anything support that goal? What is the best way to help your patient in this situation? Or: If you don't admit your mistake and your mistake comes to light, what will happen to you then?

#3 "I'm a doctor/I'm a nurse.... I can't afford to make mistakes."

Consider: Can you afford to miss out on learning, self –awareness and reflection? What have you learned from past mistakes? How many people do you know who are perfect? How many people do you know who have never, ever made a mistake?

What do you say when someone comes to you to tell you they have made a mistake? What is most important to you in that situation?

CHAPTER EIGHT

Your ultimate plan for action

The big recruitment checklist

Recruitment is one of the key drivers for profit and loss in any care service. Providers often use KPI figures showing current occupancy levels, sickness and absence levels, agency percentages, training attendance, work related absence / non-work related absence, number of open vacancies, starter and leaver trends to determine where their money goes. When you attend board meetings, you will find there will be a heated debate how to reduce costs, achieve regulatory compliance and improve quality all in the same time. It is a delicate balancing act with all eyes on professionals involved in recruitment to come up with a plan to recruit more good people for less cash. All of this is happening on the backdrop of alarming statistics predicting a rapid decline of qualified workforce numbers coupled with a projected rise of opportunities for new services to meet demand.

The success of your recruitment campaigns is often judged solely on the ability to recruit sufficient numbers of staff. However, this approach does not provide you with the information you really need to inform your strategy or support you in achieving your departmental goals.

The following assessment breaks down all stages of the recruitment process. It analysis each element in detail to give you clarity of successful components as well as areas of development potential.

Start: Operational -and clinical background assessment

- What are your current priority goals in terms of recruitment?
- What are your key challenges?
- Where do you spend the most time and resources during the recruitment process?
- Ideally, how would you want this to change in future?
- What parts of the recruitment process are working well? What aspects are you looking to improve?
- Do you foresee planned and emergency admissions having a significant impact on your staffing levels?
- What is your average timeframe to fill a vacancy?

Stage 1: Locate your candidate

- How many vacancies do you currently have for qualified / unqualified staff?
- How many staff are you looking to recruit part–time / maternity cover / flexi-bank?
- How many applications do you want to give you a good choice of applicants?
- How many people would need to see your advert to generate this number?
- How far would people be willing to travel for the position on offer?
- How many people live in your catchment area?
- How many care providers are based in your catchment area?
- How many of those cater for similar clientele and therefore likely to target similar candidates?
- How many care providers in your area offer higher salaries / better benefit packages?
- How long is your process from advertising the vacancy to induction start date?

Stage 2: Engage your workforce

- Have you identified a target market or audience for your vacancies?
- What is the estimated number of people exposed to your advert?
- How many people take action after seeing your advert?
- How many people do you realistically need to reach through online / offline marketing?
- What advertising channels are you currently using online and offline?
- Which channels are most effective in generating suitable applicants?
- Which channels are the most resource intense? (Time/Money/Personnel)
- What marketing strategies would you consider to be the best value for money options?
- Which channels do you actively use to build an applicant pipeline / contact database?
- What systems do you have to measure the effectiveness of each advertising channel?

Stage 3: Assess your candidate

- What is the percentage of suitable applicants following the initial screening of all applications?
- What tools do you use to support your selection process? (i.e. Screening assessment tools)?
- Who is involved in writing interview questions for each position?
- Who is involved in the interview and selection process?
- Who would benefit from being involved in the selection process?
- What are your attendance rates for assessment centres/recruitment days/interviews?
- What is the percentage of applicants offered a position compared to number of unsuitable candidates?

Stage 4: Negotiate with your candidate

- Who is involved in presenting your organising during the recruitment process?
- Have you got the peers of candidates for the relevant vacancies involved?
- Have you got a structured and planned pitch in place for each staff group you are looking to employ?
- How would you rate the effectiveness of your pitch on a scale of 1-5?
- How many candidates on average negotiate their salary?
- How many candidates on average ask for other benefits such as training as part of their starting package?
- What do you offer apart from salary benefits to secure a candidate?
- Do you plan and prepare for the negotiation process?
- Are you able to achieve your goals during negotiations?

Reading Room

A lot of companies now use electronic reading rooms as a tool for informal networking. I really love the idea of employees share the titles of the books helping them thrive in business and in life. Here is a list of my favourite books. Enjoy!

Abraham, Jay 'Getting Everything You Can Out Of All You've Got'
Truman Talley Books, 2000

Borg, James 'Persuasion'
Prentice Hall, 2011

Brown, Rob 'How To Build Your Reputation'
Ecademy Press, 2007

Burchard, Brendon 'The Millionaire Messenger'
Simon and Schuster, 2011

Carnegie, Dale 'How To Win Friends And Influence People'
Simon and Schuster Reissue, 1998

Cassell, Jeremy and Bird, Tom 'Brilliant Selling'
Pearson Education Limited, 2012

Cialdini, R.B. Ph.D. 'Influence: The Psychology Of Persuasion'
Harper Business, 2007

Covey, Stephen, Ph.D. 'The Seven Habits Of Highly Effective People'
Macmillan, 1997

Diamond, Stuart 'Getting More'
Portfolio Penguin, 2011

Gallo, Carmine 'Talk Like Ted'
Pan Macmillian, 2014

Hsieh, Tony 'Delivering Happiness'
Business Plus

Priestley, Daniel 'Key Person Of Influence'
Rethink Press, 2014

Schaefer, Mark "The Tao Of Twitter'
McGraw-Hill Education, 2014

Smith-Courtenay, Natasha 'The Million Dollar Blog'
Piatkus, 2016

Tracey, Brian 'The 6-Figure Speaker'
Brian Tracey International, 2016

Before you go…

Are you a little sad that you have reached the end of this book already?

Actually, it's not really the end! I have put together a library filled with videos, event news, free online course and plenty of other recruitment –and retention resources to help you fill your vacancies in no time. You can access it here: www.goagencyfree.com

Writing this book has been a great journey for me filled with many challenges, obstacles and victories. I would love to hear your thoughts and feedback. You can contact me here: heike@thecoachingnurse.com. I respond to all my e-mails personally.

As a thank you for reading my book, I am offering you a 10% discount!

I know reading the book is not the same as live training coming straight to your place of work. I am pleased to offer you a 10% discount on all live events and online training courses. Just quote 'Recruitment' when you get in touch for your 10% discount.

You can find more staff recruitment –and retention coaching tools on my website: www.goagencyfree.com

Warm wishes,
Heike Guilford

Dover, 2016
PS: I really hope you have enjoyed this book. Please share your feedback for future readers on Amazon. It really makes a difference. Thank you so much!

About the author:

 Heike Guilford is an experienced coach and qualified nurse with a special interest in recruitment and retention. Her career in healthcare has taken her from Support Worker to Head of Department before setting up her own thriving coaching practice. Heike has presented her work at local – and national conferences. Heike is a regular guest writer for industry specific publications.

16192246R00040

Printed in Great Britain
by Amazon